ARE YOU A PUZZLE MASTER?

Professor Halliwell, the world's leading expert on rare and exotic animals, is baffled. He does not know what a tigrus is— or where the animal lives. But, with the help of his good friends Susan, Tom, Matt and their little dog Patches, he's determined to find out.

Join these five adventurers in a fantasy-filled safari for the tigrus that will take them to the wildest places on Earth. Along the way, they'll meet fierce tigers in India, polar bears in the Arctic and crocodiles in the Everglades of North America.

Help the Professor, Tom, Susan, Matt and Patches solve the many puzzles, mazes and challenges on their safari. These include finding animal oddities, lost objects and hidden creatures. They all lead up to the toughest challenge of all—solving the mystery of the tigrus.

Answers in the back of the book

Published 1992 by Joshua Morris Publishing,
a subsidiary of The Reader's Digest Association, Inc.,
4 North Parade, Bath BA1 1LF.
Copyright © 1992 John Speirs
Storyline, Gill Speirs
All rights reserved. Unauthorized reproduction,
in any manner, is prohibited.

British Library Cataloguing-in-Publication Data.
A catalogue record for this book is available
from the British Library.
ISBN 1-85724-962-3
Printed in France

John Speirs
PUZZLE MASTERS
Safari for the Tigrus

JOSHUA MORRIS PUBLISHING

MUDDLE MAZE

Tom, Matt, Susan and Patches arrive at Professor Halliwell's sprawling research room inside the university museum. Here the Professor collects thousands of notes on wild animals for the books he writes.

Just now the Professor is excited about one animal in particular, an animal that no one has ever seen before—the tigrus.

"Hello!" calls a voice from somewhere deep in the confusion. "I'll be ready to go in just a minute ... once I find a few more things. Oh, dear! Everything was here just a minute ago!"

"Professor!" calls Susan. "Can we help you find what you're looking for?"

"Certainly," answers the Professor. "Come over to my desk. It might be easier to start looking from here."

Can you find the shortest route to Professor Halliwell? Trace your way to him through the mountains of clutter. Then find your way out again, collecting—in this order—the four passports ( ), camera, video camera, picnic basket, maps, telescope, compass, the four suitcases, binoculars, the Professor's favourite green umbrella, butterfly net and his spectacles.

CREATURE CLUTTER

"Here's something you don't see every day," says the Professor proudly. "This is a painting of 25 different wild animals. It was created by local artists who borrowed my research cards."

"I think they should look at your cards a little more closely next time," says Susan. "Hmm, at least they left a space for the tigrus."

"Oh, have you met Squawk, my pet parrot?"

asks the Professor. "Oh, no! I've lost the tickets."

In painting the wild animals, the local artists have made some mistakes. Each of the 25 different animals has something wrong with it. Can you find the mistakes? And where are those tickets? The places that the Professor and his friends will visit are hidden in the picture frame. Can you break the code to find out where they are going?

TIGER TRACKING

Professor Halliwell, Tom, Susan, Matt and Patches ride an elephant into the tall grass of the Indian interior. Flying ahead of them is the Professor's pet parrot, Squawk.

"*Tigrus* sounds a little like *tiger*, don't you think?" asks Professor Halliwell. "I think we have a good chance of finding the tigrus here in the land of the tiger."

BOOM bada BOOM bada BOOM go the drums of the beaters the Professor has hired.

"I hope these beaters can round up all the tigers," says Professor Halliwell. "Then we can photograph them

and see if the tigrus is among them."

"If I were a tigrus," says Matt nervously, "the last place I'd want to be is with all these tigers."

Guide the Professor and his friends through the tall grass to photograph each tiger face to face. You'll know you're on the right path when all the letters in the flashes from the camera spell out a secret message. What is it? Here's a clue: —H— T-G--- I—O— W—HT-E —ND-- --G---. M—E O—. *The beaters have to collect the 39 used flashbulbs before leaving. Can you help the beaters find them?*

INTO AFRICA

"Wow! Look at all those animals!" says Susan, peering down.

"Don't lean out *too* far," warns Professor Halliwell.

They are ballooning along the Great Rift Valley in Africa.

"Do you see a tigrus?" asks the Professor hopefully.

"I'm not quite sure what a tigrus looks like," says Matt.

"It looks like no other animal you've ever seen before," says the Professor. "So if you recognise all the animals you see, none of them is a tigrus."

"I can see some animals that will be in big trouble if they don't start running soon!" says Tom.

"Can you believe it?" sighs the Professor. "Now I've misplaced the compass!"

Most of these animals wouldn't hurt a fly, but ten of them are savage hunters stalking their prey. Can you find those ten? Can you also pick out three identical zebras? And, while you're at it, would you please look for the compass Professor Halliwell has lost?

MONKEY BUSINESS

"Whew!" pants Matt, wiping his brow. "We must be in the biggest sandbox in the world!"

"You're right," says Professor Halliwell. "This is the Sahara, in northern Africa. It is the largest desert on Earth."

"Look!" cries Susan. "What's that up ahead?"

"It's an oasis!" says Tom.

"Maybe the tigrus is up there, keeping cool in the shade!" shouts Matt. "And look at that water. I'm going swimming!"

"Not so fast!" says the Professor. "That pool of water is probably a mirage. Oh, bother! If only I could find my spectacles and binoculars, I could get a better look at it."

The Professor is right—it is a mirage. There are four differences between the top left side and top right side of the mirage. There are also 15 differences between the reflections in the water and what's above them. Can you spot all 19 differences? And where has the Professor left his spectacles and binoculars?

ARCTIC ADVENTURE

"Iceberg ahead!" shouts Susan.

A huge mass of ice rises up out of the freezing North Pole mist.

"There are animals all over it!" cries Matt.

"If only one were the tigrus," shudders Tom, "then we could go somewhere warm."

"No time to think of that!" declares Professor Halliwell. "We must get

around that iceberg and through these ice floes or we won't make it to our base camp. The temperature is dropping fast, and these ice floes could freeze together and block us in."

Help the Professor and his young friends find the shortest waterway to their North Pole base camp in the distance.

Can you see 11 different kinds of Arctic animals here?

Squawk, the Professor's parrot, hates the cold. Can you see where he's hiding to keep warm?

SWAMP SEARCH

"I feel sure the tigrus lives somewhere in the swamp," says Professor Halliwell confidently.

"How do we get through here?" wonders Susan. "All the waterways look the same."

Sssssssss!

"Is there a hole in our raft?" asks Tom in alarm.

"That isn't the sound of hissing air," says the Professor. "That's the sound of a hissing—"

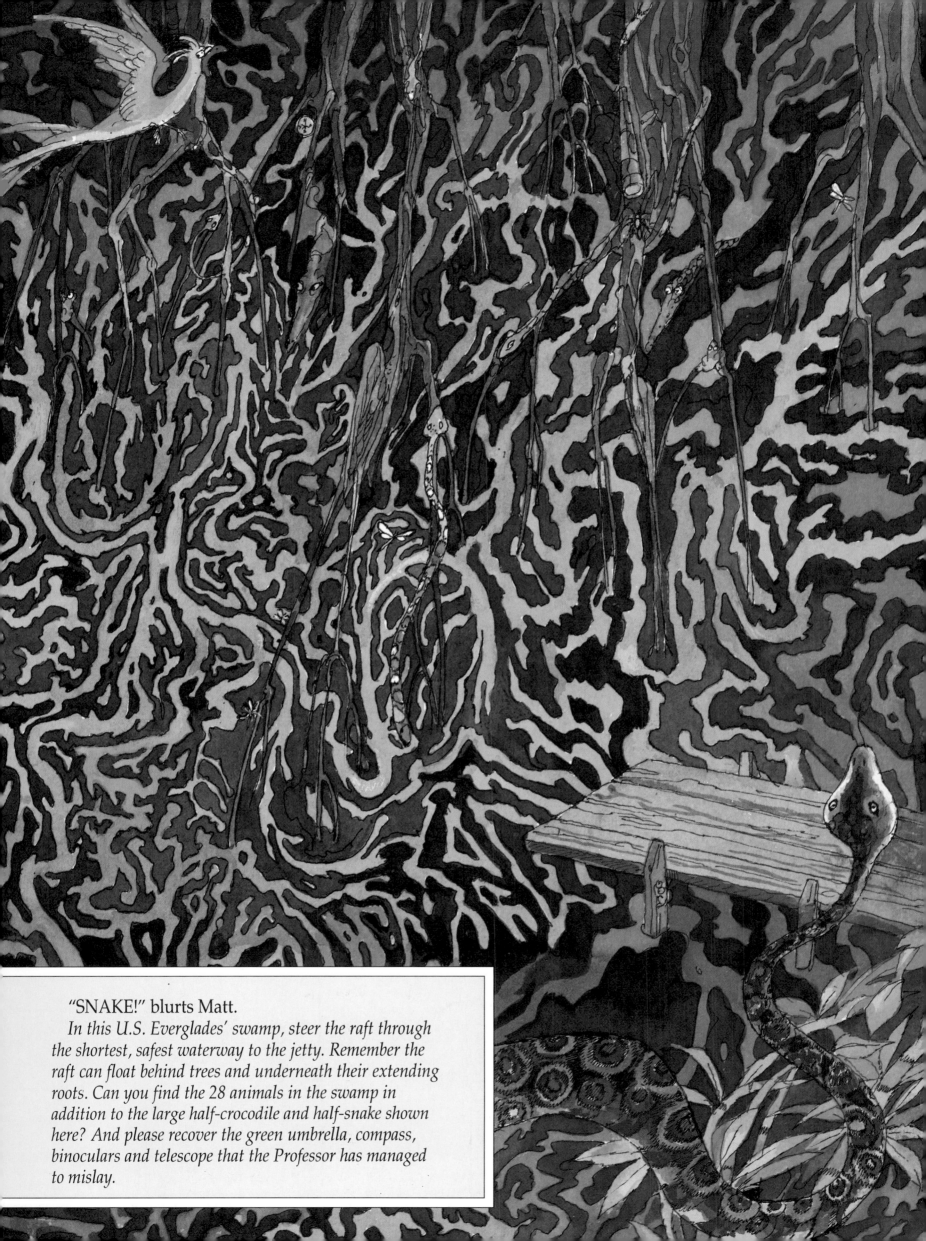

"SNAKE!" blurts Matt.

In this U.S. Everglades' swamp, steer the raft through the shortest, safest waterway to the jetty. Remember the raft can float behind trees and underneath their extending roots. Can you find the 28 animals in the swamp in addition to the large half-crocodile and half-snake shown here? And please recover the green umbrella, compass, binoculars and telescope that the Professor has managed to mislay.

TROPICAL TANGLE

Through the steaming heat of a South American rainforest, the bold explorers press forwards.

"We need to find the Inaqua tribe," says the Professor. "They live here and know all the wild animals of the rainforest."

"I see lots of animals," says Susan. "But I don't see any Inaqua."

"Maybe that tree-house is where their chief lives," says Tom, pointing upwards. "Let's look."

"But how are we going to get up there?" asks Matt. "The only one of us who can fly is Squawk."

"Um, has anyone seen my binoculars?" asks the Professor. "Oh, dear! The last cheese sandwich is missing—and my umbrella!"

The Inaqua can see their visitors even though their visitors can't see them. Can you spot the 25 Inaqua? Help the Professor and his friends follow one long vine to the tree-top home of the Inaqua chief. Where are the three things the Professor has lost?

BENEATH THE GREAT BARRIER REEF

Down, down, down sinks the diving bell carrying the Professor, Tom, Susan, Matt, Patches and Squawk. They are searching for the tigrus deep in the waters of Australia's Great Barrier Reef.

"If this tigrus is a sea creature," says the Professor, "it'd be quite at home down here."

"*Eeeew!*" says Matt. "Look at all those slimy sea snakes!"

"They're not snakes," says the Professor. "They're moray eels."

"Well, there are more morays than you can count!" says Tom, amazed.

Can you find three identical moray eels as well as the moray eel that is swimming in the opposite direction to the others? Squawk, the Professor's parrot, doesn't like being underwater. Where is he hiding?

HOMEWARD BOUND

Professor Halliwell, Susan, Tom, Matt, Patches and Squawk have arrived home by ocean liner.

"It would have been a perfect safari ... if we had found the tigrus," sighs the Professor. "I'm sorry to have taken you on this wild goose chase."

"Don't you mean a wild *tigrus* chase?" jokes Matt. "That's okay. I wouldn't have missed this trip for anything!"

"Me neither!" says Tom.

"Nor me!" says Susan.

"Um, do any of you have the passports?" asks the Professor.

"No!" answer Tom, Susan and Matt together. "You always keep them!"

They all run off in different directions looking for them.

Search the crowd to find Tom, Matt, Susan, Patches, Professor Halliwell and Squawk. Can you find the four passports? Somewhere over the dock are three identical sea gulls. Can you pick them out?

EUREKA!

"How did you first learn about the tigrus, anyway?" Susan asks the Professor back at the museum.

"The artists who painted the wild animals said they saw it on one of my research cards," answers the Professor.

"You see, I always put pictures of animals, along with their names, on the cards. But my office is so messy that I don't think I could find the tigrus card easily."

"We'll help you find it!" say Tom, Matt and Susan together. They each reach for a handful of cards at the same time. "Oops!" they cry, as the cards fly up into the air.

"Look," says Susan. "These cards are very strange. There's one with the back of an alligator and the front of a walrus."

GATOR

TIG ER

OST

BRA

ELE

GATOR

ON

ELE

PHANT

ZE BRA

WAL

ER

CH

ELE

ELE

RUS

OST

TIG

RUS

RICH

"I guess that makes it a gatorwal," laughs Matt.

Susan snaps her fingers. "Quick! Collect the cards and put them in order. I bet two together will tell us what a tigrus is."

Do as Susan says—put the Professor's odd-looking research cards in order. Starting with the large single tiger card, match all the cards to make up complete animals, using each card only once and ending with the large, single walrus card. You can use coins or buttons to mark the cards you've used. Can you now solve the mystery of the tigrus? Here's a clue: turn over the facing page and slide it slowly over this page. Can you also find the Professor's green umbrella, compass and spectacles?

PUZZLE ANSWERS

Muddle Maze

You can find the shortest route to Professor Halliwell by following the RED path. The BLUE path will take you out again. Circled in BLUE are the things you need to collect. They are—in order—the four passports, the camera, video camera, picnic basket, maps, telescope, compass, the four suitcases, binoculars, the Professor's favourite green umbrella, butterfly net and his spectacles. Did you find everything?

Creature Clutter

The animal mistakes are circled in RED. They are a duck with chicken feet, an elephant with a bushy tail, a walrus with upside-down tusks, a camel with three humps, a polar bear with rabbit ears, an alligator with webbed hind feet, a hippopotamus with a horn, a rhinoceros with a unicorn horn, a zebra with a long mane of hair, an armadillo with a long tail that is bushy at the end, a flying ostrich, a giraffe with three antlers, a moose with deer spots, a kangaroo with a pouch on its back, a bat with a beak, a tiger with a lion's mane, a lion with a sabre tooth, a turtle with a single back flipper, an eagle with long tail-feathers, a warthog with four tusks, a chimpanzee with a tail, a platypus in a tree, a rhesus monkey with no tail, a shark with two top fins and a penguin with long legs. The tickets are circled in BLUE. Beginning with the letter "I" in the lower left corner (indicated by the arrow), spell out every other letter in the frame, going around it twice. The letters spell out: INDIA, AFRICA, AUSTRALIA, NORTH POLE, SAHARA, SOUTH AMERICA and NORTH AMERICA. Those are the places the Professor and his friends will be visiting.

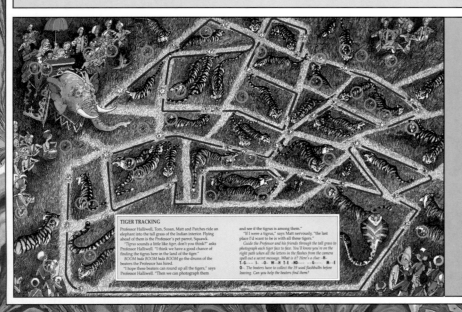

Tiger Tracking

To photograph all the tigers face to face, follow the RED path. The secret message is: "THE TIGRUS IS NOT WITH THE INDIAN TIGERS. MOVE ON." The 39 used flashbulbs are circled in BLUE.

Into Africa

The ten savage hunters stalking their prey are circled in RED. The three identical zebras are circled in BLACK. Professor Halliwell's compass is circled in BLUE.

Monkey Business

The four differences between the top left side and the top right side are circled in RED and BLUE. The 15 differences between the reflections in the water and what's above them are circled in RED. The spectacles and the binoculars are circled in BLACK.

Arctic Adventure

To find the shortest waterway to the North Pole base camp, follow the RED path. Ten different kinds of Arctic animals are circled in BLUE and numbered as follows:

1. wolf	3. weasel	5. goose	7. rabbit	9. mouse
2. hare	4. seal	6. walrus	8. caribou	10. owl

The eleventh different kind of Arctic animal is the polar bear, many of which can be seen here. Squawk is circled in BLACK.

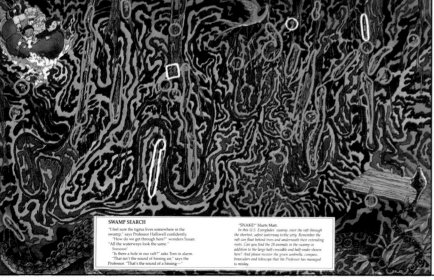

Swamp Search

To find the shortest, safest waterway to the jetty, follow the RED path. Apart from the large half-crocodile and half-snake, there are 28 swamp animals, all circled in BLUE. The green umbrella, compass, binoculars and the telescope are circled in WHITE.

Tropical Tangle

The 25 Inaqua are circled in BLUE. You can get to the tree-top home of the Inaqua chief by following the vine outlined in RED. The cheese sandwich, the binoculars and the umbrella are circled in BLACK.

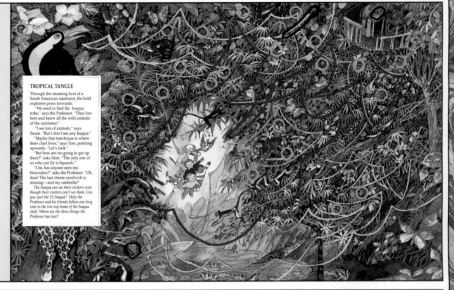

Beneath the Great Barrier Reef

The three identical moray eels are circled in RED. The moray eel swimming in the other direction is circled in BLUE. Squawk is circled in BLACK.

Homeward Bound

Tom, Matt, Susan, Patches, Professor Halliwell and Squawk are circled in BLUE. The four passports are circled in BLACK. The three identical sea gulls are circled in RED.

Eureka!

The correct sequence of the cards is numbered in RED, 1 to 27. When you slide one page slowly over the other, the letters TIG and the letters RUS will meet, forming TIGRUS. When the local artists originally painted the mural, they spilled some paint. Two of the cards—TIGER and WALRUS—stuck together, spelling out TIGRUS. And so the Professor and his friends were off on a wild tigrus chase! The green umbrella, the compass and the spectacles are circled in BLUE.